VERTICAL

gardening

**a complete guide to growing
food, herbs, and flowers in small spaces**

VERTICAL

gardening

a complete guide to growing
food, herbs, and flowers in small spaces

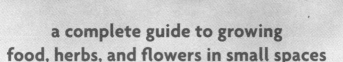

J A S O N   J O H N S

GroundSwell Books
Summertown, Tennessee

Library of Congress Cataloging-in-Publication Data

Names: Johns, Jason, author.
Title: Vertical gardening : a complete guide to growing food, herbs, and
    flowers in small spaces / Jason Johns.
Description: Summertown, Tennessee : GroundSwell Books, [2019]
Identifiers: LCCN 2019007470 (print) | LCCN 2019015495 (ebook) | ISBN
    9781570678349 (ebook) | ISBN 9781570673757 (pbk.)
Subjects: LCSH: Vertical gardening.
Classification: LCC SB463.5 (ebook) | LCC SB463.5 .J64 2019 (print) | DDC
    635—dc23
LC record available at https://lccn.loc.gov/2019007470

We chose to print this title on sustainably harvested paper
stock certified by the Forest Stewardship Council®, a
global, not-for-profit organization dedicated to the
promotion of responsible forest management worldwide.
For more information, visit www.fsc.org.

MIX
Paper from
responsible sources
FSC   FSC® C005010
www.fsc.org

Cover and interior design: John Wincek
Stock photography: 123 RF, Shutterstock

Printed in the United States of America

GroundSwell Books
an imprint of Book Publishing Company
PO Box 99
Summertown, TN 38483
888-260-8458
bookpubco.com

ISBN: 978-1-57067-375-7

24 23 22 21 20 19   1 2 3 4 5 6 7 8 9

CONTENTS

I grow plants for many reasons:
to please my eye or to please my soul,
to challenge the elements
or to challenge my patience,
for novelty or for nostalgia,

but mostly for the joy
in seeing them grow.

DAVID HOBSON

CHAPTER 1

What Is Vertical Gardening?

A vertical garden utilizes supports (such as fences, trellises, or walls) either to train plants to grow upright or to hold containers of plants above the ground. Increasingly, people see vertical gardening as a way to grow their own food in a limited space or to enjoy the benefits that plants bring to an indoor environment. Perhaps they live in a city apartment or in a townhouse with little to no outdoor room for a garden, or they have a small garden space that cannot be expanded. Some people want to save money by growing their own produce or look forward to the health benefits that come from eating fresh food and being active outdoors. There is also growing concern about how our environment is impacted by the amount of fossil fuels needed to transport food from farm to table.

Growing vertically is the answer to all these concerns, and I consider it to be one of the most exciting developments in horticulture.

1

The world is struggling to support a growing population, and vertical gardening could provide a much-needed solution for boosting productivity without increasing tillable acreage. Better productivity would discourage deforestation, a serious problem in developing countries that are struggling to produce enough food for consumption and export.

Many people refer to vertical gardening as urban gardening because it's popular in cities and towns where growing space is at a premium. Anyone who has a balcony or a small yard can turn it into a productive vegetable garden by growing plants in pots. However, even if you do have space for a garden, you might want to grow more produce than you have room for. (You're torn between planting those pumpkins or a dozen rows of carrots!) Instead of having to forgo a crop you'd love to try, what if you grew it upright? By gardening vertically, you can use arbors, arches, fences, trellises, walls, and pots to create more growing space. You can even grow vertically to increase the amount of growing space in your greenhouse.

I love showing off my vertical space to friends and fellow gardeners. Their eyes positively light up as they realize how much produce they can grow in a small area! Let me relate briefly what is possible.

In a three-foot-square area of my garden, I can typically grow up to nine strawberry plants if I space them properly. Last year, I built a vertical strawberry planter that fit in that same space. It held seventy-two strawberry plants with plenty of room for all of them, and they flourished! Best of all, they were easier to harvest and maintain than plants grown in the ground.

Why Gardening Makes You Happy

Working with the soil and growing plants can provide significant benefits to your sense of well-being. Longtime gardeners, myself included, often claim that gardening helps alleviate depression and makes them feel happier.

In recent years, scientists have discovered a link between working with soil and lower levels of depression. Friendly bacteria in the soil have an effect on the human brain that's similar to antidepressants. Researchers from Bristol University and University College London (both in England) have discovered that a bacteria commonly found in soil, Mycobacterium vaccae, stimulates brain cells to create serotonin. Serotonin is the chemical that elevates mood. Most antidepressants work by stimulating the production of serotonin or by helping it bind to chemical receptors in the brain. So, improve your day by getting your hands dirty!

One of my favorite summer vegetables is cucumbers; they're lovely in a salad or sandwich. However, these plants vine freely, take up a lot of valuable ground, and attract slugs and snails. When I grow cucumber plants vertically, I can grow three plants on a trellis or netting in only four square feet of soil. Vertically grown cucumbers are straighter and have softer skins than those I grow along the ground, and they don't suffer anywhere near the same amount of slug and snail damage.

Pumpkin vines can grow at least fifty or sixty feet long, limiting what else you can plant in that space. When I grow pumpkins along the ground, I have to pinch the ends off the vines and continuously reposition them so they don't crowd out other plants. It's a lot easier to keep them under control if they're grown vertically, and training the vines to grow up a wall frees up valuable real estate in my garden.

The Advantages of Growing Vertically

Whether you live in the city or the suburbs, you can maximize your productivity and grow your own vegetables, fruits, flowers, or herbs by creating a vertical garden. Even if you have a garden you're able to expand, applying vertical gardening techniques will help you grow more produce without having to work up more ground.

If only a small portion of your yard or terrace receives adequate sunlight, you can set out large containers in this area or fix smaller containers or trellises to walls or fences to take advantage of the exposure you get. Gardening in containers is also

helpful if you don't have good soil in your growing space. You can purchase commercial garden soil or create your own mix. (See page 52 for my favorite blend.)

You can plant in virtually any container that will hold soil and tolerate exposure to water. For instance, if you're feeling more whimsical than practical, you can create planters out of old rubber boots with drain holes fashioned in the soles. If you're feeling handy, you can drill large holes into a wide PVC pipe, cap the ends, fill with soil, then fix the pipe to a wall or fence to grow strawberries or other shallow-rooted plants. This process can also be used with old gutters.

Arbors, arches, and pergolas work well in larger gardens, allowing you to grow climbing plants or even attach pots for smaller plants. These structures can become a feature of your garden, and a seated arbor with scented plants on it provides a lovely place to sit.

Attractive fruit and vegetable plants will also add visual interest to a garden, patio, or yard. Look at the colorful flowers found on cucumbers, squashes, or runner beans. Even the fruits can be eye-catching. What about growing violet-podded French climbing beans, purple-podded peas, or yellow, orange, or striped tomatoes?

Epic Vertical Gardens

Vertical gardening on a large scale can be quite impressive. Outside New Street Station in Birmingham, England, is a huge vertical garden, about 2,700 square feet in size and containing over twenty-five different types of plants—a welcome splash of color and greenery in an otherwise drab city center. I've also heard about a gardener in the US who's growing thousands of lettuce plants in over-the-door shoe organizers that he's hung on fences. In Florida, there are greenhouse growers who combine vertical gardening with hydroponics to grow massive amounts of fresh produce (typically lettuces and herbs) in tiny areas. In Malaysia, Singapore, and Thailand, vertical gardens are installed on the exteriors of buildings to provide much needed greenery.

Weeds are less likely to grow in a vertical garden. If you start out with a sterile growing medium, the only weeds that will take root will come from seeds that blow in on the wind. Also, plants in vertical gardens tend to be more densely planted than in horizontal gardens, making it more difficult for weeds to get established. If weeds do develop, they're easy to remove because the soil will be quite loose.

Finally, anyone who suffers from back or mobility problems will find a vertical garden ideal because they won't have to bend over as much to care for their plants. I love being able to tend my garden while standing up and not having to bend over or crawl around.

What You'll Learn about Vertical Gardening

As you read this book, you'll learn about everything from planning a new vertical garden space to incorporating vertical structures into your current garden. I'll teach you how to maximize the use of your space and build a vertical garden as cheaply as you want. (You might be surprised how little investment you'll need to get an attractive, highly productive garden.) I will also show you how to determine the best place for your vertical garden in order to make the most of your sun exposure, protect your plants from wind, and arrange your plants so they'll grow harmoniously.

I wrote this book to share my passion for vertical gardening with you. It's a fantastic way to boost your productivity and maximize the yield from the space you have. By the time you've finished this book you'll be able to create your own gorgeous, high-yielding garden.

CHAPTER 2

Choosing Plants

With a little imagination, you can grow almost any plant vertically, although some plants are more suited to this than others. A good way to choose what to grow is to start with the foods you eat regularly. Even a single plant can provide a surprisingly large yield, so you may not need much of any one crop to have all you can eat through the growing season. Consider growing a few plants of different types, so you don't end up with a glut of any one thing. Many people enjoy a variety, from salad vegetables and vining tomatoes and cucumbers to perhaps winter squash or even potatoes.

Think beyond how some plants are traditionally grown. Instead of vining tomatoes, consider varieties of tomatoes that do well in hanging baskets. Peas are usually grown up a fence, but you can also grow them in hanging or mounted containers so the pea vines will grow over the sides. Strawberries will also grow well in hanging baskets or containers on walls. They'll create a pretty display, and if you use different varieties, you can enjoy berries throughout the growing season.

Here are some characteristics to consider when choosing plants for a vertical garden.

- **DEPTH OF THE ROOTS**—Plants with shallow roots are best because they can be grown in small containers that can be easily mounted to a support. If you want to grow plants with long roots, plant them directly into the ground or in large containers that are placed on the ground, and then grow them up a wall or fence.

- **HEIGHT**—Tall plants are not well suited for growing vertically because they're susceptible to wind damage. Although these plants can be supported, it can be tricky to use a support that's sufficiently sturdy, particularly in a shallow container; you will need a wall or fence to attach them to. Grow them directly in the ground or in a sheltered location where they won't be damaged by high winds, such as in front of a wall.

- **TRAILING HABIT**—Trailing plants generate a gorgeous display of color as they grow over the side of a container. You can also train them to grow up a fence or trellis by tying them to supports.

- **CLIMBING HEIGHT**—Climbing plants can be grown up a wall, fence, or garden structure, such as an arch, pergola, or trellis. Because many of them reach a significant height, it's better to plant them directly into the ground. If you grow them in containers, they may struggle to reach their full potential. (That may actually be a plus if you want to limit their size; just be aware of the extra attention that container plants will require to stay well watered and fed.) Climbing plants are either self-climbers (they can attach themselves directly to a wall or to a trellis) or they require support. Grapes are very attractive when grown over an arch or pergola; wisteria is often grown along the wall of a house.

- **SIZE OF FRUIT**—Special consideration needs to be given to plants that normally grow along the ground. They may not be well suited if they produce large fruits; the weight of the hanging fruit may damage stems or vines. You can fashion small hammocks to support the growing fruit, but large fruit, such as giant pumpkins, squashes, or watermelons, will likely strain your supports beyond capacity. Plants that bear a lot of fruit, such as high-yielding tomatoes, will need extra support so their branches won't snap under the weight.

Vegetables

Cucumbers are a great vegetable to grow vertically, because they're often straighter and have softer, thinner skins than cucumbers that have to defend themselves from the abuse of life on the ground. When cucumbers are grown beyond the reach of slugs and snails, they'll suffer much less damage.

Beans, melons, small pumpkins, and small winter squash will also grow well in a vertical garden, though if the fruits are going to be larger than a volleyball, keep the vines on the ground instead. (See pages 36 and 40 for information on supporting smaller squash and melons.)

Salad vegetables, such as beets, lettuces, radishes, red onions, spinach, and spring onions (scallions), all have shallow roots, so they'll grow well in a vertical garden. They're a good choice if you want to use containers fixed to a wall. Radishes and lettuces grow very quickly, so you can sow multiple crops in a single container. You can also use succession planting, where you plant a few seeds every couple of weeks to have a continuous crop rather than a sudden glut.

As mentioned earlier, peas can also be grown vertically. They're actually much easier to harvest when they're hanging down from

a container. You don't have to bend over to harvest the pods, and it's more difficult for mice and rabbits to reach them.

Although you can't train root vegetables to grow in any other direction but down, you can still grow them in planters attached to walls or large containers on the ground. Opt for shallow-rooted vegetables, such as radishes or globe carrots. Larger shallow-rooted vegetables, such as leeks and onions, will work as long as you provide ample space between them.

Deep-rooted vegetables, such as carrots and parsnips, are not as well suited for growing in a vertical garden because of the size planter required to accommodate their roots. For example, the combined weight of these vegetables and the soil needed to grow them is usually too much for most supports. Grow them directly in the ground and train the vines up some supports.

Steer clear of the non-leafy brassicas—broccoli, Brussels sprouts, cabbage, and cauliflower. They're not well suited for a vertical garden because the plants themselves become so large and heavy. You're better off growing these directly in the ground or in containers placed on the ground.

Bear in mind that tall plants, such as tomatoes and beans, will require some support. Runner beans will need something to climb up, and broad beans may be exposed to damaging winds if grown above ground level. See more information on specific supports on pages 33–41.

Herbs

Herbs are beautiful anywhere in a vertical garden, but they're particularly useful if you locate them next to a door near your kitchen so you can pick them while cooking. (Be aware that marjoram will attract a lot of bees, so this may not be the best herb to grow near a window or door!) Herbs are also a logical choice for an indoor living wall (see page 54). With a bit of careful planning, you can easily create a wonderful vertical herb garden that not only looks great but smells divine too.

Almost any herb will work in a vertical garden, as most of them are still small when full grown and will flourish in attached containers. Larger herbs, such as lavender, rosemary, and sage, can be grown in a vertical garden, but you need to prune them regularly to prevent them from becoming leggy and overgrown. Herbs such as cilantro, dill, and fennel can grow up to six feet

tall, making them susceptible to wind damage. These are best located in sheltered locations or tied to supports.

Herbs such as basil, cilantro, and dill are annuals, but chives, oregano, rosemary, sage, and tarragon are perennials—unless winter temperatures are particularly harsh in your area. If you're fortunate enough to live in a climate that has mild winters, you may be able to keep some annual herbs going for more than one season, especially if you can keep them next to a wall that gets lots of sunlight and protects from harsh winds.

Fruits

F ruits are very popular to grow in a vertical garden, and some fruit-bearing plants thrive in containers. Others don't do as well because of the above-ground space they require or the deep roots they develop.

Strawberries and pineberries (white strawberries with a pineapple flavor) are ideal for a vertical garden because they have shallow roots. They grow very well in mounted gutters or small containers that can be fixed to a wall or fence. Traditionally grown strawberries will send runners along the ground, exposing the berries to slugs and snails, but growing them in a vertical garden will protect them from this damage. (You may have to use netting to protect them from birds.)

Vine fruit, such as grapes, and vining varieties of blackberries, loganberries, and raspberries do very well in containers; locate them in front of a sturdy fence or wall for support. A variety of blackberry has recently been developed specifically for hanging baskets.

Trees, even dwarf varieties, typically don't do well in a vertical garden because they need a lot of space for their roots. However, you can grow them against walls or fences and train them using a process known as espalier or fanning that flattens the tree against a fence or wall. (This is most commonly done with apples.) Training a fruit tree like this allows for a good crop of fruit without the tree taking up the amount of space it would if untrained. It requires patience, as a tree won't attain the desired shape and produce a good crop for a few years.

Shrub fruit, such as blueberries, black and red currants, and raspberries, won't produce fruit when grown in containers unless they can get to be a good size. They're also more prolific if they're pruned into a bowl shape to increase air circulation, so they may be too large for your small space.

Ornamental Vines and Flowers

Flowering vines or brightly colored displays of flowers in containers provide stunning beauty to an otherwise drab wall or fence. With careful planning, you can create a continuous array of color throughout the growing season. Bushes and shrubs might overwhelm a vertical garden, but if properly pruned back, they can be grown along a wall or fence either directly in the ground or in large pots.

Ornamental vines, such as clematis, passion flower, and wisteria, are usually trained up a wall or fence. It will take a few years for them to reach a sizable height, but the pleasing visual effect is well worth it. See pages 10, 31, and 70 for information on siting and caring for ornamental vines.

Smaller flowering plants, trailing flowers (such as lobelia), and flowering bulbs will work well in any vertical garden, although you need to be able to reach them easily so you can remove spent flower heads and perform other maintenance.

Some bulbs, such as dahlias, are not frost hardy and will need to be dug up and stored in a frost-free environment over the winter. When planting flowers, remember to group plants with similar soil and care requirements together in a single pot. (See more information on page 52.)

Best Plants for a Vertical Garden

FRUITS

NAME	SUNLIGHT NEEDS	SOIL TYPE	GROWING NOTES
Blackberries	Full sun (will tolerate light shade)	Deep, fertile, well drained, moisture retaining, slightly acidic	Tumbling varieties are now available. Large vines will need support. Thornless cultivars tend to produce the best fruit.
Blueberries	Full sun, sheltered from wind	Well drained, acidic	Will need support in exposed areas. Opt for dwarf varieties and keep well pruned. Large bushes do not thrive when cut back.
Currants	Full sun (will tolerate light shade)	Fertile, well drained, moisture retaining	Opt for dwarf varieties and keep well pruned. Tie to supports.
Gooseberries	Full sun (will tolerate light shade)	Well drained, moisture retaining	Opt for bush or dwarf varieties and prune annually. Very susceptible to sawfly.
Grapes	Full sun, facing south or west	Well drained	Need support and regular pruning. Ideal for growing over a pergola.
Kiwi	Full sun, sheltered from wind, facing south or west	Fertile, well drained, slightly acidic	Tie large vine to support. Check hardiness for your area.
Melons	Full sun, sheltered from wind	Fertile, well drained	Tie vines to supports. Opt for varieties with small fruits. Larger fruit may need individual supports.
Passion Fruit	Full sun (will tolerate light shade), facing south or west	Fertile, well drained, moisture retaining	Tie large vine to support. Only eat when fully ripe.
Raspberries	Full sun (will tolerate light shade)	Fertile, well drained moisture retaining, slightly acidic	Varieties with short canes will be easier to manage. Will need support in exposed areas and requires pruning every year.
Strawberries	Full sun (will tolerate light shade)	Fertile, well drained	Shallow-rooted plant ideal for gutters, pipes, bottles, or other shallow containers. Will grow in hanging baskets. Keep well weeded, even after harvest season.

VEGETABLES

NAME	SUNLIGHT NEEDS	SOIL TYPE	GROWING NOTES
Arugula (rocket)	Full sun, but tolerates partial shade	Fertile, well drained	Shallow-rooted plant that can be tricky to germinate.
Beans, broad	Full sun	Well drained	Will require support in exposed areas. Can be grown through mild winters. Susceptible to blackfly and aphids, as well as fungal diseases.
Beans, climbing	Full sun	Deep, fertile, slightly acidic	Great for trellises; require support. In cooler areas, pinch the growing tips when the stems are 8 to 9 feet high.
Beans, dwarf	Full sun	Deep, fertile, slightly acidic	Grow well in shallow containers. Plants do not require support, and some will hang over the edge of baskets.
Beets	Full sun	Fertile, well drained	Ideal for shallow containers. For best texture, harvest between 1½ to 2½ inches in diameter.
Carrots	Full sun	Very sandy, free of rocks; does not like heavily manured soil	Globe varieties are ideal for shallow containers. Long varieties require deeper containers. Can be grown individually in pipes. Grow with onions or garlic to prevent carrot fly.
Cucumbers	Full sun	Fertile	Self-supporting climbers but will benefit from ties. Grow well on a trellis or pergola. Choose quick-maturing varieties in cool climates.
Garlic	Full sun	Well drained, alkaline	Suitable for shallow containers. Best planted in October or November as it requires cold to form ample bulbs. Ensure good spacing to prevent fungal diseases.
Leeks	Full sun	Fertile, well drained	Suitable for shallow containers. Susceptible to a variety of diseases. Can be grown over the winter in many areas.
Lettuce	Partial shade	Moist, well drained	Suitable for shallow containers. Many varieties will tolerate some cold. Susceptible to slug and snail damage.
Onions/ Shallots	Full sun	Well drained, alkaline	Suitable for shallow containers. Can be grown over the winter.
Parsnips	Full sun	Deep, loose	Require deep containers to grow properly. Difficult to germinate. Best harvested after the first frost.

NAME	SUNLIGHT NEEDS	SOIL TYPE	GROWING NOTES
Peas	Full sun	Well drained, alkaline	Shallow-rooted plant. Natural climbers, though will trail from hanging baskets. Sow when soil is warm.
Peppers, bell, chile, sweet	Full sun	Fertile, well drained, moisture retaining, slightly acidic	Require support and plenty of sun. Need warm temperatures; grow quick-maturing varieties in cool climates.
Potatoes, sweet	Full sun	Moist, well drained	Grow as a vine and can be trained up a trellis. Provide shelter from wind.
Potatoes, white	Full sun	Deep, fertile, moisture retaining; will break up clay soil, but loose soil produces higher yields	Require deep containers (buckets or bags). Not suitable for growing on walls or fences.
Radishes	Full sun, but tolerates partial shade	Fertile, moisture retaining	Shallow-rooted plant that matures very rapidly. Great to plant with slower growers. Harvest when small.
Rutabaga	Full sun	Fertile, well drained, moisture retaining, will tolerate heavy soils	Shallow-rooted plant with large leaves.
Scallions	Full sun, but tolerates partial shade	Fertile, well drained	Shallow-rooted plant that grows quite slowly.
Spinach	Full sun (benefits from partial shade when hot)	Fertile	Shallow-rooted plant that matures rapidly. Some varieties will overwinter.
Squash, winter	Full sun	Fertile, well drained	Mostly long vines, though some varieties are bushing. Most will grow upward, though benefit from ties. Opt for varieties with small fruits if possible. Large fruits will require individual support
Swiss chard	Full sun (benefits from partial shade when hot)	Well drained, moisture retaining	Shallow-rooted plant that matures rapidly.
Tomatoes	Full sun (will tolerate light shade)	Fertile, well drained	Tumbling varieties are ideally suited to hanging baskets. Vining varieties require ties; bush varieties can be grown in containers. Fruit requires heat to ripen.
Turnips	Full sun	Firm, fertile, alkaline	Shallow-rooted plant with large leaves.

FLOWERS

NAME	SUNLIGHT NEEDS	SOIL TYPE	GROWING NOTES
Air plants	Bright shade	Usually grown on wood, shells, or rocks	Ideal for indoor living walls. Require regular misting and good ventilation. Not usually cold tolerant.
Begonias	Full sun (will tolerate light shade)	Fertile, well drained	Move tubers indoors before the first frost and store indoors until weather warms.
Bulbs	Full sun (will tolerate light shade)	Well drained	Crocus, daffodils, hyacinths, and tulips come in a wide variety of types and colors. Can be grown in containers with other plants. Do not overwater.
Ferns	Light to heavy shade	Moisture retaining	Suitable for living walls and hanging baskets.
Geraniums	Full sun (will tolerate light shade)	Well drained	Good in hanging baskets. Remove dead flowers to encourage more blooms.
Hostas	Partial to full shade	Fertile, moisture retaining	Foliage will range from dark green to variegated. Very susceptible to slug and snail damage. Will grow to full size in three to four years.
Impatiens	Partial to full shade	Well drained, moisture retaining	Can be planted around other plants in containers. Very sensitive to lack of water and full sun.
Ivy	Partial to full shade	Loose, well drained	Vines will attach to walls and fences and can cause damage.
Nasturtiums	Full sun	Well drained, moisture retaining	Leaves, flowers, and seeds are edible. Will self-seed. Very easy to grow. Attract aphids and blackfly.
Pansies	Full sun	Fertile, well drained, moisture retaining	Can be planted around other plants in containers. Don't like extreme heat but will tolerate near freezing temperatures.
Primroses or Primula	Full sun (will tolerate light shade)	Well drained, moisture retaining	Prefer a sheltered location, perfect for growing under trees.
Succulents	Full sun (will tolerate light shade)	Poor, well drained	Ideal for indoor living walls. Can be densely planted to make an attractive display.
Viola	Full sun (will tolerate light shade)	Well drained, moisture retaining	Vining varieties are ideal for hanging baskets. Can be planted around other plants in containers. Can survive mild to cold winters.
Wallflower	Full sun (will tolerate light shade)	Moisture retaining	Some varieties are perennials; others are biennials, flowering in their second year. Can grow several feet tall. Keep well watered, particularly during the flowering season.

HERBS

NAME	SUNLIGHT NEEDS	SOIL TYPE	GROWING NOTES
Basil	Full sun (will tolerate light shade)	Fertile, well drained	Grows well with tomatoes; enhances the flavor of the fruit. Not cold tolerant.
Bay leaf	Full sun (will tolerate light shade)	Well drained	Prune and train to keep small. To avoid root damage, do not overwater.
Chives	Full sun (will tolerate light shade)	Well drained, moisture retaining	Grow near carrots to repel carrot fly. The flowers attract bees, so it's best not to grow near a door or window.
Cilantro	Full sun (will tolerate light shade)	Fertile, well drained	Will grow very tall. Root requires a deep container. Grow in full sun to produce seeds. Water regularly to avoid premature bolting. Doesn't like to be transplanted.
Lavender	Full sun	Poor or moderately fertile, well drained	Prune and train to keep small. Very fragrant, attracts bees.
Lemon balm	Full sun (will tolerate light shade)	Well drained, moisture retaining	Will spread easily; grow in containers.
Marjoram	Full sun	Loose, well drained	Prune and train to keep small. Attracts bees. Not cold tolerant.
Mint	Full sun to full shade	Any type	Will spread easily; grow in containers.
Oregano	Full sun (will tolerate light shade)	Loose, well drained	Some varieties will stay green all winter.
Parsley	Full sun (will tolerate light shade)	Well drained, moisture retaining	A biennial (will overwinter and flower the next year).
Rosemary	Full sun, ideally south, west, or east facing.	Well drained, moisture retaining	Prune and train to keep small.
Sage	Full sun, sheltered location	Well drained, moisture retaining	Prune and train to keep small. Do not overwater.
Thyme	Full sun	Well drained	Will grow quite large. Trailing varieties are ideal for hanging baskets.

CHAPTER 3

Setting Up a Vertical Garden

The very first step in planning your vertical garden is to evaluate your space and any structures that are already there. You might be surprised at how much room you actually have when you think about how every inch of space can be utilized. That small, drab wall could easily provide enough support for the production of a few dozen heads of lettuce and twenty pounds of strawberries! You can be as elaborate or as simple as you want. Even a small space with a few containers can be the backdrop for your creativity.

How many square feet are available for containers? What structures can you attach containers to? Do you need to build something or can you use an existing fence, pergola, trellis, or wall? If what's there is in poor condition, can it be repaired so you can use it? Is it strong enough?

How permanent do you want your vertical garden to be? If you're renting, you'll want structures that are easy to move. Depending on the way the sun tracks across your garden, you may want to move your containers around during the day or through the seasons to maximize their exposure to sun. You also might want to move your plants to a sunroom or greenhouse in order to protect them over the winter.

Consider the ownership of the structures too. If your neighbor has put up an attractive fence, they may not appreciate you drilling holes into it to attach containers. The same would go for the wall of their building. Do you have room to build something next to your neighbor's fence or wall that you can use?

Be sure to consider the entrance to your vertical garden. Can you turn this into a growing space? An archway over the entrance could support squashes or cucumbers and produce a colorful, productive display. You might also hang shade-loving plants underneath.

Tips for Vertical Garden Design

Because you'll have a limited amount of room, you'll need to carefully plan what you're going to grow in order to maximize your space. You may also need materials to construct your supports, and if you plan in advance, you'll have everything on hand when you start.

CHOOSE WHAT TO GROW

As I mentioned earlier, the most practical way to decide what produce to grow is to take stock of what you and your family enjoy eating. Grow the fruits and vegetables that you regularly use. Unless you're an experienced gardener, start with small quantities of a variety of plants, so you won't be overwhelmed with more produce than you can keep up with. If you're planning on creating a display of flowers, think about what you can plant that will give a good display of color throughout the year.

The productivity of garden spaces, even those close to each other, may differ, so a vegetable that thrived for you in one garden might not do as well in a neighboring one. In addition, harvests will differ somewhat from year to year. Peppers may do well in your garden for many years but fail to do so in a particular year for any number of reasons. Be prepared to test conditions in your new spot to find the optimal place for each plant.

Next, determine which of your favorite fruits and vegetables can grow in your area. If you live in a northern latitude, it will be difficult to grow plants such as bell peppers, eggplants, or watermelons, which require a long growing season and warm weather. If you live in a hot climate, it will be challenging to grow lettuce and other greens unless you regularly get a few months of cool temperatures.

Make a list of all the plants you want to grow, then note when they need to be sown and harvested; the amount of time between those dates is the length of the growing season they require. You can compare this to the dates of the first and last frost in your area to determine whether you can grow those plants; this information is widely available online. (If you're able to grow vertically inside a small greenhouse, you'll be able to raise plants that wouldn't tolerate outdoor conditions where you live.)

EVALUATE YOUR SUN EXPOSURE

Sunlight, along with good soil and adequate water, is a basic requirement for growing any plant, and it will play a significant role in what you can grow in your space. For instance, tomatoes need lots of sunlight, while lettuce might require partial shade if summers in your area are hot.

You'll need to be aware of where and for how long the sun tracks across your garden in order to know what you can grow. A tree might provide shade to protect delicate plants during the heat of the day, or it could prevent your plants from getting the light they desperately need. In urban areas, shade from buildings and walls can hamper the growth of your plants.

I used to live in a home where a neighbor's wall was high enough to block sunlight from reaching my backyard until late afternoon. That amount of shade limited what I could grow in the ground. However, I noticed that the top of a wall opposite my neighbor was high enough to catch the sunlight during a good part of the day. By fixing containers where the sun hit this wall, I was able to site my plants to reach the sunlight that was available.

Another thing to consider is the height of the sun in the sky. Depending on how far away from the equator you are, this can vary considerably. An area that has a lot of sun in the summer could become shady quite quickly as winter approaches and the sun dips lower in the sky.

If you're new to the area, trying engaging your neighbors on the subject, especially if they're also gardeners. There's a good chance they can share their years of experience tracking the sun where you live. (They may also be able to advise you about what grows best in that area and what pests and diseases to watch for.) Alternatively, there are now fairly sophisticated websites and apps you can use to determine the sun's path any time of year, anywhere in the world.

Trees and permanent structures may not be the only things that can block sunlight; as your larger plants grow taller, they could cast shade over shorter plants. If you're going to grow plants of varying heights and you live in the northern hemisphere, you might want to site tall plants on the northern side of your garden; the opposite is true in the southern hemisphere where tall plants will cast less shade if they're on the southern side.

If you're lucky enough to have a particularly sunny spot, you can also use shade to your advantage. Site delicate lettuce and shade-loving flowers where larger plants will offer protection from the sun, especially during the middle of the day when the sun's rays are most direct. This strategy will enable you to get the most variety from your garden space. Also, if you're using growing containers that are portable, you can adjust the locations of your plants according to the height of the sun.

CHECK AVAILABILITY OF WATER

The most ideal situation is having a source of water from an outdoor spigot nearby. If you're planning to water by hand, consider how you're going to fill a watering can and how far you'll have to carry it. If your water source is close enough, using a garden hose to water containers is handy as long as you can use a stream of water that's gentle enough not to displace any soil or plants.

If you're planning to create an automatic irrigation system, an outdoor water source is a must. That source also needs to be close enough to the location of your irrigation system to ensure good water flow. Ideas for different types of irrigation systems can be found on pages 64–67.

Using a rainwater collection system is not only an ecological solution, but it also might be imperative if no good outdoor water source exists, an indoor water source is not practical, or you plan on being out of town for any amount of time during the growing season. See page 63 for some ideas for installing a rainwater collector.

SEE WHERE THE WIND BLOWS

Be aware that plants grown vertically are going to be more susceptible to wind damage than plants growing along the ground. Tall or vining plants may reach above your head. Trellises and arches could be blown over, damaging your plants and possibly even your property. If you have the flexibility, site your vertical garden where it will be protected from prevailing winds. Keep in mind that you can get some pretty strong wind eddies around walls. Arbors, trellises, and other structures should be securely fixed to the ground or a wall to hold them in place.

If you live in a region prone to high winds or heavy storms, consider plants that are wind tolerant. Low-growing plants, such as lettuce and strawberries, will hold up better than unwieldy squash vines with their large leaves. You'll also want to make sure that any structures in your vertical garden are particularly sturdy and secure. See page 42 for more information on considerations for growing in windy areas.

LOCATE AN EASY ACCESS

Be sure to consider how you're going to get to all parts of your vertical garden to water and feed your plants, put in new plants, fend off pests and disease, and harvest produce. Hanging out a bedroom window to get to plants is not the safest idea, and using a ladder against a wall filled with closely spaced containers is asking for trouble. The best access point will depend on where you've sited your vertical garden and the space you have available.

Also take into consideration how you're going to move yourself and your gardening equipment around either a fully mature vertical garden or plants placed directly in the ground. You may be carrying a watering can or other equipment into the garden, so ensure you can do that without causing any damage to your plants. It's very easy to knock flowers or fruits off plants, which is something you'll want to avoid. There's a tendency for people to put up hanging baskets at just the right height for someone to walk into them—or to place them above doorways so that after watering, they drip down on anyone coming out the door!

Years ago, I built some raised beds, made sure there was space between them for my wheelbarrow, and happily planted them. It was only when the plants grew that I suddenly realized my nice wide paths were only wide if there were no plants growing next to them! A lot of the plants had grown out over the paths, and I was no longer able to get a wheelbarrow between the beds without breaking stems or tearing off leaves. It may be difficult to envision that tiny seedling as a ten-foot vine, so make sure any paths around your vertical garden are wide enough to accommodate the size of mature plants.

PLAN OUT YOUR PLOT

Some people can't be bothered with planning and would rather purchase a few containers, wing it, and hope for the best. But you'll be more efficient and get excellent results if you take the time to plan the best placement for containers and plants. You'll also keep costs down because you'll be less likely to spend money on containers and compost you won't need. If you're building structures or fixing containers to walls, it's better to have a game plan in advance so you can minimize the need to take something apart and redo it.

Measure your growing space, then draw a scale model on paper. This will help you visualize the environment and how it will look, as well as determine the size and shape of containers that you will need. Graph or squared paper is a great tool for this. If you count out a certain number of squares for every foot of space, your drawing will give you an accurate rep-

resentation of the size of existing structures and the placement of trees, pathways, and beds. With a clear picture in front of you, you'll get a more realistic sense of what will fit where. You can also fashion containers to scale using cut-out paper shapes and move them around on your grid until you find the optimal layout.

Where you position individual containers and plants will depend on the eventual size of a plant, the amount of sun and shade it needs, and the size container its roots will require. Take the list of plants you matched to your growing season, and note the size they will attain in your area. (That impatience will get much bigger with a long growing season than it will where summers are short.) Draw in a representation on your scale model that matches how large your plants are predicted to become. When you're done, you'll want to envision your garden at maturity to ensure everything is going to fit, that you've calculated for appropriate access, and your plants will have enough room to breathe. If you don't have sufficient air circulation, your plants can't dry out properly after being watered or rained upon, and mold and fungus can develop.

Also consider how quickly your plants will grow. You can use the space around the base of a slow-growing plant to produce a crop from a fast-growing plant and increase your productivity. I will often plant radishes and carrots together, because the radishes mature sooner than the carrots. You can also employ a concept known as succession planting to replace an early-maturing plant with another plant that also doesn't require much time to grow. I grew early potatoes, which I harvested in late June. I then planted rutabagas and turnips, which I started to harvest in October.

Plants that enjoy heat, such as bell peppers, chiles, and eggplants, do very well at the base of a wall where the wall itself creates a pocket of warmth and reflects heat back onto the plants. As mentioned earlier, use tall plants to cast shade on plants that don't appreciate long periods of direct sun, such as lettuce and parsley. Because of the sheer size of ornamental vines, it's best to plant them directly in the soil. Containers won't provide enough room to accommodate root growth or adequate watering.

If you're planning to grow everything in containers, you might consider planting different types of plants in one container. Be sure to combine plants that have the same soil needs. There's no point growing a plant that likes damp soil with one that likes dry soil; either both plants will do poorly or one won't survive. Likewise, if a plant likes an acidic soil, don't pair it with one that likes alkaline soil. (See more on types of soil on pages 51–53.)

Be patient with this stage of planning. As you go along, you'll have realizations and acquire information that will alter your initial plans, and you'll have to reshuffle your scale model. Allow time for the creative process to evolve. Set your plan aside and come back to it later with fresh eyes.

Special Consideration for Siting Herbs

If you decide to grow herbs, you'll want to use them regularly, harvesting as you need them. Burying them at the back of your vertical garden or high up on a wall will make access more difficult. If you can, locate them as close to your kitchen as possible, especially if you have access from your kitchen through an exterior door or can create a living wall in or near your kitchen (see page 54).

When creating a herb garden, use separate planters for each herb if possible. This allows you to tailor the soil conditions to each plant. Position the planters so each herb will get the amount of sun it likes. Shade-loving plants can be toward the bottom of your arrangement, out of direct sun. Plants that

like the most water can also be put toward the bottom, beneath other plants, so when you water the plants above, any excess water will drip onto the moisture-loving plants below.

If you need to grow herbs together in a container, be sure to group plants that have similar soil and sunlight needs. For example, basil appreciates a lot of heat and regular watering, but not too much water. Thyme doesn't like a heavy soil and will die if it becomes waterlogged, but it will grow with sage, which likes the same type of soil. However, thyme is not a good part-

ner for basil. Basil loves heat, but will soon wilt without enough water. Marjoram, oregano, rosemary, sage, and thyme will flourish in the same pot because they all like dry soil. Basil, cilantro, parsley, and tarragon are preferred container mates, as they need damp soil.

You can avoid the challenges of grouping herbs with opposing soil and water needs by planting them in small pots and placing the small pots in a larger container to create an attractive display. Decorate the top of the pot with colored stones or gravel to hide the fact there are multiple pots!

Supporting Your Plants

Walls and fences are popular supports for vertical gardens, but there are other supports you can utilize that will provide visual interest and give you more options. Arbors, arches, pergolas, and trellises are often found in garden areas or yards. Traditionally, they're used for growing climbing flowers, such as clematis, honeysuckle, jasmine, and roses. What if you used them to grow delicious fruit and vegetables instead? Imagine entering your garden, not through an archway of roses, but an archway of cucumbers or squashes!

Deciding which supports to opt for will depend on the space you have, what you'd like to grow, and the time, money, and skills you have if you need to build something. Even if you plan to use a fence or wall for support, you may need to fix wooden battens or a trellis to it to provide a better surface for attaching containers or vines and to increase air circulation.

You can buy ready-made supports from most garden centers, or you can construct your own if you feel your building skills are adequate. Ready-made supports are usually made of wood; treated wood will last for several years. Coated metal supports are very durable as long as the coating remains intact, but they're susceptible to damage and rust. I haven't found plastic supports to be rigid or strong enough to support the weight of a plant with fruit, unless the supports are small and used with relatively small plants.

If you make your own supports, you can fashion something affordable that will be the perfect size and shape for your space. There are many plans for different types available online, and a number of them are quite easy to construct.

In the section that follows I'll focus on three general types of supports: trellises, pallets, and permanent structures. Then I'll pass on suggestions for how to attach containers and plants, as well as share special considerations if you're supporting plants in windy conditions.

TRELLISES

A trellis is an ideal support for any climbing or trailing plant, giving them lots of surfaces to grip onto as they climb. Some trellises are so substantial they can be entirely free standing, but most are light enough they can easily be fixed to a wall or fence. They're ideal for climbing beans, cucumbers, honeysuckle, jasmine, and squashes. You will need to tie up

tomatoes or broad beans, but climbing beans, peas, and other self-supporting plants will grip a trellis without assistance.

Trellises are also good if you plan to grow climbing or vining plants in large containers placed on the ground at the base of a wall. It's difficult to insert a single support deeply enough into a container that it will remain upright when the plant is fully grown. Fixing a trellis to the wall behind the container will provide the support needed to bear the weight of the plant without the container toppling over.

You can also plant squashes and other vining plants on a succession of small trellises attached together to form upside-down Vs. The plants will grow up and down the trellises, taking up a lot less space than they would normally, so this is an ideal method for anyone who has limited space but wants to grow a vining plant. You can even manage giant pumpkins using this method, positioning the vines as they grow to ensure the fruits are at the bottom of each V, where it meets the ground.

Whether you use a trellis made of wood, metal, or plastic depends on your budget and personal preference. If you're on a tight budget, you can fashion a trellis out of metal chicken wire or plastic netting strung between two wooden struts or attached to a rectangular wooden frame. You can also build trellises out of bamboo canes tied together at the top with string to form a tipi or even more simply by tying twine between two posts for plants to grow on.

As with any support or container, ensure there is about an inch gap between the trellis and any fence or wall behind it so that air can circulate. This will reduce the chance of mold or rot on the wall from the moist environment created by your plants.

PALLETS

One of my favorite ways to grow vertically in a garden is to use pallets. They're usually set up against or fixed to a standing structure, such as a wall or fence, but they can be free standing if they're secured into the ground using long, sturdy stakes.

The arrangement of slats used to make pallets enables you to grow plants with different needs on a single structure. You can set containers into the spaces created by the slats or fill those spaces with soil and grow plants directly in them. You can also fix containers to the pallets, much as you would a wall or fence. Paint both the pallets and containers to make a colorful, eye-catching display.

Pallets are often available for free from companies that receive or transport goods by truck. These companies are usually grateful to have them hauled away, as they often have to pay to dispose of them. Driving around any industrial area will often reveal numerous pallets put out with the trash. Pallets are also great for building compost bins and many other garden structures. People have even built sheds with discarded pallets!

ARBORS, ARCHES, AND PERGOLAS

Permanent garden structures, such as arbors, arches, and pergolas, add architectural interest to any garden or yard. Arches are often used over entrances, but they also make great covers for pathways. If you have space, a seated arbor in a corner of a

garden can allow you the luxury of resting indulgently amid the fruits (or vegetables) of your labors.

Pergolas can also provide lovely shaded seating areas. They're ideally suited for any plant that climbs but are most commonly used for grapes. In many Mediterranean countries, small crops of grapes are traditionally grown on pergolas, and families sit in the shade of their grape vines to enjoy meals and socialize.

Not only can permanent structures be used for climbing plants, you can also attach containers to them. If you're handy and adventurous, you can make these structures yourself. However, most people find it more practical to purchase them ready-made.

Attaching Plants to Supports

When you're growing vertically, you may want to attach plants to supports to encourage them to grow upright. Twine is an option for tying up plants, but I find pipe cleaners are even better. The fluffy exteriors of pipe cleaners protect your plants from damage, and you can reuse them season after season, which generates less waste and creates less stress on the environment. You can also easily loosen them as your plant grows, so they don't become too tight and cut into the stem.

When tying your plants, work carefully and use a figure eight around the stem and the support, crossing the eight between them. This will help prevent any damage to your plants.

Depending on what you grow, you may need to provide support for the fruits as well as the plants. Cucumbers are small enough to hang without breaking their stems, but even average-sized melons and pumpkins will need something underneath the fruits as they grow. Most vertical gardeners attach hammocks, ledges, or bars above or behind the vines for larger fruits to rest on or hang from. Whatever material you use for support (especially for a sling or hammock), make sure that water can't pool in

Building Your Own Vertical Garden Planter

A wire mesh against a wall is ideal for tall or climbing plants. The mesh provides a framework for you to tie the plants to and gives them the support they need. You can also use the mesh to hang various containers. If the containers have handles, you can use hooks to move them around the mesh as the needs of your plants change. You can even use the mesh simultaneously to support both containers and climbing plants; the plants in the containers will provide interest as your climbers are filling in the space.

Build a frame around the area you plan to cover using two-inch wooden battens. The battens will hold the mesh away from the wall to allow air flow and prevent mold and other diseases. You may also need to put a batten in the center of the mesh to keep the mesh from sagging. Use galvanized metal mesh; it not only looks attractive but will resist weathering for many years.

Securing the frame to the wall with screws will provide more strength than using nails. Staple the mesh to the frame, making sure the mesh is as taut as possible so it will support the weight of your plants. Then hang your containers on the mesh, or train your plants to grow up it.

it; standing water will attract pests and rot the fruits. Many vertical gardeners use pantyhose because the mesh material they're made from is usually strong and permeable. Another option is to grow small varieties of melons, pumpkins, and squashes. A pumpkin variety such as Munchkin or Jack-O'-Lantern would be ideal, where Atlantic Giant would be much too large.

If you're supporting fruits, check the plants occasionally to make sure there's no damage to the stems or support structure. The weight of a large crop can pull a side stem away from the main branch. In years where you get a bumper crop, you may have to thin the fruits or provide extra support to prevent branches from snapping. Tomatoes, for example, can sometimes produce so much fruit that the trusses supporting them start to pull away from the stems. Whatever you use, remember that it has to be strong enough to support not just the fruits but the weight of the vine too.

Dealing with Wind

I f you live in an area that's susceptible to strong winds, be especially careful to anchor supports so they'll hold up under duress. Be sure to tie up plants securely so they're not blown about.

If your area is at risk for tornadoes or hurricanes, you'll need to take special precautions. Besides doubling down on your efforts to secure supports, consider making your vertical garden removable, so you can take down containers and store them safely before high winds arrive. Loose containers can become dangerous projectiles during an intense storm.

Even if extreme weather is not usually a problem for you, most locations will experience high winds at least once a year. High winds can damage tall plants, breaking stems and dislodging fruits and flowers. Place tall plants in sheltered areas, and tie them to trellises or other supports to prevent stems from snapping.

Containers and Planters

Y ou've done the work of planning your garden, and you know what you need. Now you can start acquiring the materials to build your vertical garden and begin putting them all together.

You may decide to grow a few of your plants directly in the soil, but a good bit of vertical gardening takes place in contain-

ers. Think beyond the traditional flowerpots, hanging baskets, and landscaping containers you see in garden centers. Literally, anything deep and sturdy enough to hold soil can be used as part of a vertical garden.

Personally, I like making my own containers from recycled items, as the process of making them is fun and eco-friendly. You can grow

shallow-rooted plants, such as radishes or strawberries, in something just a few inches deep. Used plastic bottles also make superb containers. Cut a hole into them about half the length of the bottle, cap the bottle, fill the bottle with soil, and hang it horizontally with wire or sturdy twine.

You can also cut the tops of used plastic cartons and hang them from a fence to make a hanging basket. The possibilities are limitless, so the choice comes down to your budget, creativity, time, and the size of your growing area.

Ensure all of your containers have drainage holes at the bottom. This will prevent the containers from becoming waterlogged and rot the roots of your plants.

Commercial containers will usually come with drainage holes; if there aren't any or you're fashioning your own containers, drill or cut some yourself. If the container has no drainage and is made of heavy metal, pottery, or other solid material that's difficult to perforate, place some pebbles at the bottom and insert a smaller container with drain holes inside. You'll still need to drain it after a heavy rain.

HANGING BASKETS

One of the easiest ways to create a vertical garden is with hanging baskets. They're sold anywhere you can get garden supplies or plants and are easy to mount on walls. Often these are filled with flowers to create a splash of color, but they're

equally good for growing vegetables. You can grow almost anything in them, although plants such as peas, strawberries, tumbling tomatoes, and other trailing plants are particularly well suited.

Hanging baskets can be placed indoors, on the vertical struts of a pergola or arbor, or on any wall or fence. Several hanging baskets of herbs on either side of your kitchen door will make a great kitchen herb garden.

An advantage of traditional hangers for baskets is that they extend far enough from a wall that moisture from the baskets won't usually cause the wall to rot. The downside of having baskets attached to hangers is that you'll need to shelter your baskets in a safe place whenever there are strong winds, as noted on page 42.

GUTTERS AND DRAINPIPES

Other great vertical gardening containers can be made from gutters and large plastic drainpipes. These containers are best for shallow-rooted plants. Create a dramatic effect by putting them up on multiple levels, either attaching them to stakes driven into the ground or fixing them to a wall or fence using gutter or pipe supports. Make sure whatever you attach them to is sturdy enough to support them.

The soil in any shallow planter, such as gutters or pipes, dries out very quickly and may require watering multiple times a day when the weather is hot. An automatic irrigation system (see pages 64 and 67) will make it much easier to water plants in these conditions.

Another way to use large drainpipes is vertically rather than horizontally. Cut a drainpipe about seven to eight feet long, then cut holes around the pipe, ensuring you leave space for the plants to grow. (See photo on opposite page.) Leave about two to three feet of solid pipe at one end, as most of it will be inserted into the ground.

Set the end of the pipe into a hole twelve to twenty-four inches deep, depending on the size of your drainpipe, how windy it is in your area, and how loose your soil is. For example, to provide enough support for a pipe that's six feet tall and eight inches wide, drive it about twelve inches into the ground. Pack the soil from the hole tightly around the outside of the pipe, then fill the pipe with more soil up to ground level. If the pipe shifts when you push on it, insert it farther into the ground.

Fill the drainpipe about one foot at a time with good-quality compost mixed with perlite or vermiculite to retain moisture. Insert a piece of wood into the top of the pipe as you fill the pipe to tamp down the soil. Leave an inch of space at the top to help prevent erosion of the soil at the top of the pipe and provide room for water to pool. As you fill the drainpipe, it's normal for some compost to fall out of the holes that you cut into the side. For this reason, some people prefer to assemble the pipe in the ground and fill it with compost before drilling the holes. The choice is between losing a little soil and making the pipe unstable through the drilling process.

The soil in vertical drainpipes dries out very quickly, so you might consider this easy solution for getting water to all parts of the pipe. Drill small holes every couple of inches around a piece of garden hose or half-inch plastic pipe. Place this in the middle of the drainpipe before you fill the drainpipe with soil, leaving some of the irrigation hose or smaller pipe above the top of the drainpipe so you can pour water into it. You can use a funnel when you water so more of the water will find its way down through the pipe.

PREMADE CONTAINERS

You can also purchase containers made specially for attaching to a wall or fence. They're not the cheapest option, but they will

allow you to get started quickly and easily. These containers are made of a variety of materials and vary significantly in price.

Most premade vertical planters are designed for shallow-rooted plants, such as lettuce or strawberries. The individual planting spaces hold very little soil and will only support a small plant. Bear in mind that these spaces will dry out rapidly in hot weather and will require regular watering. Be advised, as well, that premade planters have a limited lifespan and may need to be replaced in two to four years.

A wooden planter is more durable than a plastic one, but it's much heavier and will need to be fixed to a solid wall or fence. A wooden planter will be more expensive, but it will last much longer than plastic, particularly if you treat the wood with a food-grade preservative.

Even if you have a very large garden supply center near you, their selection of premade planters will be limited. Your best bet is to look for these specialty planters online. Many options are available, so you can find the best match for your gardening needs and your pocketbook.

CONSIDERATIONS FOR HANGING AND ATTACHING CONTAINERS

Here are some practical ideas to keep in mind no matter what type of container you use.

- Soil in containers will eventually become depleted of nutrients, so it's important to replace it every year. Add some pelleted chicken manure, well-rotted manure, or compost to replenish these nutrients.
- Place heavy containers at the lowest part of your garden. The farther above the ground they are, the more strain they will put on supports.
- Flimsy containers should not be put in exposed areas where the wind will damage them.
- Ensure that supports, fixtures, and hangers are strong enough to support the weight of your containers, plus the soil and mature, fruiting plants. Consider that the weight of unripe fruits could add considerably to what your supports will need to bear.

- Provide enough room for air to circulate between an attached container and a wooden wall. Even a small gap will help prevent the mold and rot that might occur when moisture is trapped between the container and the wall.

- Site the containers so you can get to them easily once they're full of plants, and make sure they don't block access paths.

- Be aware that hanging baskets and attached containers will need drainage holes and frequent watering, especially in hot weather. When container plants are fully grown, they will need watering even when it rains, as their leaves will cause the water to run away from the soil. Take into account where excess water will drip.

- Leave two to three inches between the top of the container and the top of the soil to prevent soil from washing out when it rains or being blown out by wind. If soil loss from the wind continues to be an issue, place a layer of small, light stones on top of the soil to weigh it down.

The Sole of Improvisation

One of the best inexpensive planters for a vertical garden is an over-the-door shoe hanger. It can be fixed to a wall or fence and the pockets filled with soil. A shoe hanger planter will last for a few years and is great for shallow-rooted plants, such as lettuce and strawberries. Remember to puncture some holes in each pocket for drainage, so your plants don't become waterlogged.

The Best Soil Mix for Containers

If you're growing in containers, having an appropriate soil mix is vital. Your plants are completely dependent on the soil for water, nutrients, and support, so you'll want a mix that provides these benefits. A good-quality soil will also help you get a higher yield from your container garden than you would by planting directly in the ground. Your plants will not need as much feeding, will survive better during dry spells, and will grow more vigorously.

The majority of plants like a soil that is free-draining, rich, retains water, and allows air to circulate around the roots. If your soil is also sterile—free from weed seeds, diseases, and pests—you'll have less maintenance after you plant. (The only weeds you'll encounter are those blown in on the wind.)

You can buy packaged compost and soil mixes from a garden center, but if you want to get the best possible crops, you'll need a special soil mix—possibly more than one if you're growing plants with different needs.

Different types of plants prefer different levels of soil acidity, alkalinity, and moisture retention, so grow plants with similar soil requirements in the same containers. An alternative is to put each plant in a separate pot with the soil it prefers, place the pots together in a larger container, and fill that with stones, sand, or soil.

The best soil mix I've found was developed by the creator of the square foot gardening concept, Mel Bartholomew. It's made from equal parts of the following:

- compost
- peat moss
- vermiculite

Some plants prefer a more acidic or alkaline soil than this mix will provide, and levels can be adjusted by adding soil amendments, such as lime. Preferably, the compost should come from at least five different sources in order to provide an ideal range of the micronutrients that are essential to plant growth. Finding five different types of compost may not be possible, particularly if you don't need large amounts. If this is the case, buy the best-quality compost you can afford. I usually use one or two brands of packaged compost along with some of my homemade

compost. If you're buying large quantities of compost, start with a single type and amend it with a nutrient mix.

You don't need to compact this soil mix into the containers; just gently push it so that it's firm, but not solid. When it comes time to plant, you'll just have to scoop the soil to one side with your hands,

insert your plant, and press the soil back in place. If you're planting in a windy area, you may want to put small pebbles on top of the soil to keep it from blowing away.

This mix is designed to retain water but not become soggy, which would rot the roots of your plants and eventually kill them. The vermiculite helps to keep the balance of moisture in the soil to a level that most plants prefer—just be sure to include drainage holes in your containers. This mix is also relatively light, an important factor when you're attaching containers full of soil and plants to a wall.

If you're unable to or prefer not to use this mix, combine rich, well-decomposed compost with vermiculite and some commercial slow-release fertilizer or pelleted chicken manure. Use one to two parts vermiculite to five parts compost, depending on what plants are going into the container. Peas and beans prefer moist soils with less vermiculite; carrots like free-draining soil with more vermiculite. Add the fertilizer according to the manufacturer's instructions, or work a heaping handful of pelleted chicken manure into the compost (about four handfuls per square meter).

Creating a Living Wall Indoors

One of the most interesting and unusual applications of vertical gardening is an indoor living wall. Living walls provide a sense of the outdoors, and allow you to exercise your creativity. Companies like to install them in offices because plants provide an appreciated touch of live space within structured interiors and are invigorating to both employees and visitors.

Not only are living indoor walls beautiful, they are beneficial as well. According to scientific studies conducted by NASA over the past few decades, evidence exists that tropical plants such as ferns, ficus, palms, philodendron, and spider plants can absorb volatile organic compounds (VOCs), toxic substances that are emitted into the air from glues, paints, laminate flooring, and cleaning products. A living wall in your home can become an effective biofilter that will help clean the air. Indoor plants also increase humidity levels (which

can cool temperatures in the summer and warm temperatures in the winter) and elevate oxygen levels.

Button ferns, ficus, peace lilies, red and green prayer plants, spider plants, umbrella plants, and anything from the croton family will flourish on an indoor wall. Many herbs will also work well in standard indoor light, but most vegetables will require special

grow lights in order to mature and fruit. Plants that have small root systems are ideal for living walls because of the limited growing area available to them.

Typically, a living wall is a frame built from metal or wood that is comprised of separate modules for individual plants and their growing medium. If you also install an automatic watering system, your wall can be fairly low maintenance; you don't have to remember to water regularly or risk spilling water onto floors or walls.

You can use soil or a lightweight soil substitute, depending on the type of wall you're installing and how much weight it will bear. You can also grow your plants hydroponically, with the roots entirely in nutrient-rich water—an approach that's as high-tech as it looks! Larger plants are best placed at the bottom of the wall on the outer edges, so they have more room to grow. Bushier plants work well in the center of the wall; place trailing plants toward the bottom, where they won't crowd out other plants.

You can start simply with just a few plants on a sunny windowsill or explore plans online for floor-to-ceiling creations. As long as your plants receive all the light, food, and water they need, they'll reward you with a beautiful and functional display.

CHAPTER 4

Planting and Care

T his section will give you more hints, tips, and advice on how to take care of your vertical garden. It includes information on how to start plants from seed, keep them well watered and fed, and protect them from diseases and pests.

Starting from Seeds or Seedlings

M any of the plants that are popular to grow in vertical gardens can be bought as seedlings. Seedlings have been started in greenhouses and are usually several weeks old when they come to market, ready to be transplanted into larger containers. With seedlings, you can populate your garden quickly and start to envision what it will become early on. At certain times of the year, garden shops will start selling mature plants. They're more expensive than seedlings, but they'll enable your garden to look fully grown from the start. Whatever your choice, remember to leave enough space between the plants for them to grow. What may initially look sparse will fill in before you know it and could quickly become overcrowded!

Sometimes starting plants from seeds yourself is the best bet, depending on whether you have the time and space. Many of the more unusual varieties of flowers and vegetables can only be bought as seeds, as most garden centers will only carry seedling varieties that are popular with gardeners in your area. Also, if you start plants from seeds, you'll need to begin the process early enough that you'll have seedlings ready to plant as soon as conditions allow.

I prefer raising plants from seeds because it's cheaper; a packet of seeds will typically cost no more than a single seedling. However, if I'm not going to have the time or space to start plants, I'll purchasing seedlings. In fact, sometimes I'll get a combination of the two; seedlings will be my backup plan in case my seeds don't germinate.

There are a few exceptions. It can take years for fruit trees grown from seeds to mature and produce fruit. For example, a lemon or apple tree can be grown from seed, but the resulting plant will take up to ten years to bear. If a fruit tree is in your plans, opt for a seedling or cutting. Strawberry plants will send out runners during the growing season, and you can propagate new plants by allowing these runners to grow roots.

Starting plants from seed isn't difficult, providing you understand the conditions the seeds require in order to germinate. Buy high-quality seeds to ensure you'll get a good germination rate.

You'll also need a good-quality growing medium, such as fine soil or compost. It must drain easily and be free of lumps. Seeds need a warm environment to germinate, but not necessarily light, so a warm, dark place will work fine. (Be sure to provide a light source as soon as the seeds have germinated.) Seeds from different plants require different temperatures to sprout successfully. You can purchase a propagator with a heating element installed to germinate seeds, but a warm windowsill or greenhouse will often be just as effective.

Buyer Beware!

If you get seeds from a reputable supplier, you're more likely to have good results. You're also more likely to get what you've ordered! Every year I see instances where people ordered one type of seed and got something completely different. I once bought what I thought was naga chile seeds from a small supplier, but the plants that grew from these seeds were much milder Scotch bonnet chiles.

Be particularly wary of seeds for oddly colored or oversized strawberries. The sales photos used to sell these seeds are always altered, and the seeds themselves will only result in standard strawberries.

Most people start their seeds in a multicelled seed tray, although if you have the space, you can start your seeds in larger pots to save transplanting later. Once the seeds have germinated and developed their first set of true leaves (a set of seed leaves will appear first), you can transplant the seedlings to pots. Once

the seedling roots have filled the containers they're in, transplant the seedlings into increasingly larger pots until you place them in their final location. Depending on the plant and its tolerance to the cold, this may not be until after the risk of frost has passed.

Be very careful when transplanting your seedlings; they're very delicate and can be damaged easily. Use a small trowel or kitchen fork to lift the seedlings out of the soil and create a depression in the soil where they will be transplanted. Hold them gently by their stalks, rather than by their leaves, when moving them, and support the root system. Transplant them into their new pots, fill the pot with soil, and gently push the soil down.

Water the seedlings until the soil is moist; if they have enough moisture and light, they will develop more root growth. Once the seedlings have at least three or four true leaves and outside conditions are suitable, you can plant them outdoors in your vertical garden.

Watering

Because your plants are in containers, they won't have the same access to groundwater that plants in your yard or garden will. Also, as your plants grow, their leaves will act as an umbrella, causing rain to drain away from the soil beneath them, so watering a vertical garden on a regular basis is vital if you want your plants to survive. You can do this by hand with a watering can or garden hose, or you can set up an automatic irrigation system; see page 64 for more information.

Four factors determine how much water your plants need:

- the weather in your area
- the types of plants you have
- the type of containers you're using
- the location of your vertical garden

Depending on the climate where you live, you may need to water your plants every couple of days, once a day, or, if conditions are hot or dry, several times a day. If your plants aren't particularly leafy or they've received constant rain for a while, you may actually have to drain excess water out of your containers or cover the soil with plastic so this rainfall doesn't water-log your plants.

Some plants prefer dry conditions, and others like to sit in moist soil. Small containers will dry out more quickly than large ones, and containers made of nonporous materials retain more water than porous ones. Plants in exposed areas will need more water than those in sheltered areas because they'll be subject to the drying effects of sun and wind. If your plants are against a wall, particularly one attached to a house, the heat retained by the wall during the day will also be absorbed by your containers and the soil inside them will dry out quickly.

The best time to water your plants is in the morning, which is the period when they naturally take in moisture and prepare to grow for the day. (Yes, plants do "sleep" at night.) Watering early in the day gives them access to more water and helps them pull water out of the soil so it doesn't become soggy.

If you're building your vertical garden next to your house, you can redirect your gutter downspout into a rain barrel to collect water for irrigation. If your garden is next to a separate wall or fence, you can run gutters along the top of it to a rain barrel.

Ideally, the rain barrel should be high enough that you can get a watering can under the tap at the bottom of the barrel. Some rain barrels will allow you to attach a hose, although be aware that the water pressure isn't going to be very strong unless the barrel is elevated several feet off the ground. Be sure your barrel has a screen top that will deter mosquitoes and deflect debris. (You may still have to add larvicide tablets to completely eradicate mosquitoes.) During heavy rainfalls, your barrel may overflow, so make sure you have a system for directing that overflow away from foundations and landscaping.

Sometimes you can inexpensively retrofit used food-grade plastic barrels. Make sure the barrels didn't contain any harmful chemicals that may leech into your plants. Whether you purchase a ready-made rain barrel or make your own, be aware that the water collected inside will not be safe to drink.

Although mornings are ideal, that may not be practical for you, particularly if you leave early for work. If the only time available is later in the day, avoid getting water on the leaves or between the stem and stalks to avoid fungal diseases (such as powdery mildew) or pests looking for moisture. (Whenever you water, use this time to check over your plants for disease and pest problems.)

Don't wait until your plants start to wilt before deciding to water, as certain diseases and overwatering can also cause plants to wilt. The only sure way to know if your plants need a drink is by checking the soil. Insert a finger into the soil up to the second knuckle. If the soil feels moist at the end of your finger, you don't need to water your plant. If it feels dry, give your plant a good watering until the water starts to drip out of the drainage holes. Alternatively, you can purchase an inexpensive moisture meter, providing you a quick and easy way to check your soil.

Whenever you water your plants, always soak the soil at the base of the plant rather than spray the leaves. Watering the leaves during the day can cause sun damage and promote the growth of powdery mildew. Watering the leaves can also cause runoff; the water will drain off your plant and not onto your soil. If you have plants above each other, make sure the plants at the bottom aren't getting too much water dripping from the plants at the top.

AUTOMATIC IRRIGATION SYSTEMS FOR VERTICAL GARDENS

If you live in an arid climate, you may find that an automatic irrigation system is indispensable. Even in cool climates, installing a drip system will make plant care easier. If some of your plants are too high to water by hand or are otherwise difficult to access, you'll appreciate having an automatic watering system do that work for you. The taller and larger your plants are, the more water they'll need; if you're watering by hand, you'll have to make more trips with the watering can.

It's virtually impossible to have a large, tall vertical garden without an irrigation system. When you see a vertical garden

installed on the exterior or interior wall of a commercial building, it has an automatic irrigation system built into it, because watering by hand would be too costly and disruptive.

There are many types of irrigation systems you can get. Your choice will depend on what facilities you have near your plants, what your plants require, and what you can afford. Many automatic systems require electricity to power a pump that pushes water to the plants. If part of your vertical garden is more than a few feet above the ground, your irrigation system will either need a powerful pump to get the water to that height or the water source will need to be elevated as high as the garden.

Because you're most likely tending individual plants and not a large garden area, I think a drip irrigation system is the best option. Drip systems will gradually release water over the day to your plants, ensuring they never dry out or need manual watering. These systems consist of a hose or pipe with nozzles you can insert exactly where your plants are, so water will be directed to their roots.

It can be very helpful to have a timer built into your irrigation system. You can set it to start up in the morning and turn itself off after a few minutes; inexpensive manual timers are available. If you travel on a regular basis, there are very sophisticated units that can be programmed to a variety of settings and can manage several dozen plants at a time. The ultimate in luxury might be a ready-made vertical planter with an irrigation system built right in!

If you have just a few outdoor plants, some indoor plants, or plants in a window box, there are many types of self-watering containers you can consider. Most will come with a reservoir in the bottom of the container that allows water to slowly seep to the plant's roots (though be aware that outdoor planters can fill with rainwater and flood your plants). My favorite inexpensive low-tech solution is an inverted plastic soda bottle.

Fill it with water and screw the lid on tightly. Punch one or more holes into the cap using a needle or thin nail, then turn it upside down and push it into the soil. Depending on the number and size of the holes in the cap, it will slowly drip water out over a day or more, keeping your plant moist. Use one bottle per container. You will have to fill the bottles up regularly, but using this method can be easier than manually watering your entire garden. It's also a good way to reuse plastic bottles while making your gardening chores somewhat easier. You can paint the plastic bottles to make them more attractive or less noticeable; just make sure the paint doesn't include water-soluble toxins.

WATER CONSERVATION OPTIONS

You can also reduce your plants' demands for water by adding soil amendments that retain moisture. Perlite and vermiculite are spongy or porous materials that are inexpensive and easy to find. Perlite is used more for starting seeds, and vermiculite is an excellent moisture grabber. There are also special water-

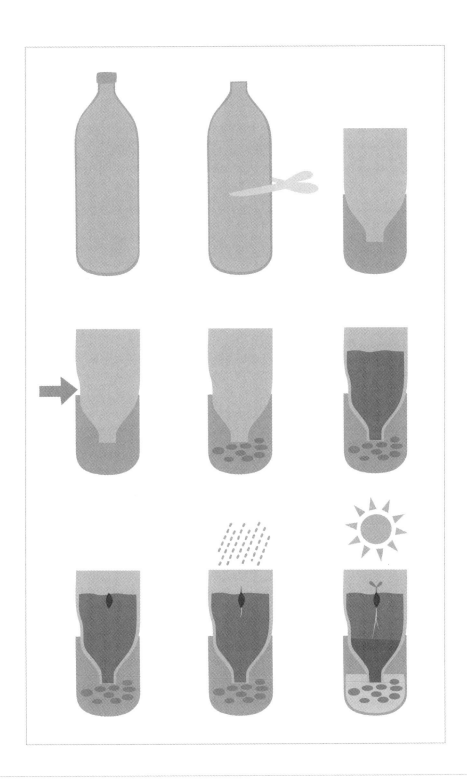

If you have any plants above eye level, you may want to use a step stool or small folding ladder, so you can easily reach the top of your plants and avoid causing any damage—to you or to them. Even a simple tear to a stem or leaf could introduce a disease that could kill your plant. Likewise, if your plants are low to the ground, you may want a kneeling pad or garden stool to make it easier to weed and harvest them, particularly if you suffer from back issues.

retention gels or water-storing crystals you can add to your soil to release moisture over time. Be sure to get something that won't break down in the soil. Covering the soil in containers with mulch or black plastic will also help retain water and prevent the soil from drying out.

When all is said and done, watering your vertical garden by hand may still be the best option for you, and it isn't the end of the world. If you can use a garden hose, you will quickly become adept at watering plants that are high up or far away. Just be careful when spraying that you don't damage your plants or wash away the soil.

Feeding Your Plants

Plants in containers need fertilizing just as plants in the ground do. If you've started them out in a good-quality compost or the soil mixture recommended on page 51, they'll get the nutrients they need for those first few weeks. After that, you'll need to supplement with plant food, especially if you're growing plants with heavy feeding demands, such as pumpkins or tomatoes. Be careful not to overfeed your plants, as that can cause a buildup of salts that will create as much damage as underfeeding; follow the instructions that came with your plant food. In winter, your plants require less food, as they don't grow as much during dark, cold months.

Commercial feeds will usually indicate the ratio of nitrogen to phosphorus and potassium in their products, often with a series of three numbers, such as 10-10-10. (The last two numbers represent the content of potash [phosphorus] and potash [potassium].) To encourage leaf growth, use a feed high in nitrogen (represented by the first number in that series). Once the plant is established and is flowering and fruiting, use a feed higher in phosphorus and potassium and lower in nitrogen. Continuing to use a high-nitrogen feed will cause a lot of leaf growth instead of flower or fruit growth. If you're growing foliage plants or greens, you can continue to use a high-nitrogen feed throughout the growing season.

Liquid feeds are easy for plants to absorb and for you to store. They usually come highly concentrated, so combine the manufacturer's recommended amount with water and apply when you water your plants. Some advanced irrigation systems can integrate liquid fertilizer, so you can add it to your system's water reservoir as directed. When your plants are young, they benefit from a dilute feed. Once they've grown, they can be fed at full strength. Check the instructions that come with your feed to determine how often and how much to apply.

Organic feeds are always my preference, and feeds made from seaweed, comfrey, or nettles contain many essential micronutrients that will benefit your plants. You can also make your own feeds, such as compost tea (see page 72). One of my favorite feeds is pelleted organic chicken manure. Scatter this on the surface of your containers; the manure will break down when plants are watered. Chicken manure does have a very distinct odor, so, depending on the location of your garden, the option of having this aroma wafting around your home may not be ideal for you.

Salts from plant foods can build up in the soil over time, making it more difficult for plants to take up moisture. To avoid salt buildup, don't feed your plants every time you water; use plain water in between feedings to flush out excess salts. Also, to prevent leaf burn, avoid getting full-strength fertilizer on leaves.

Pruning

If your plants are outgrowing their space, you might want to consider pruning them. Vegetables such as cucumbers, radishes, and beets won't need any pruning, although you will want to remove any damaged leaves. To keep tomatoes focused on fruit production rather than spreading beyond their bounds, pinch back the tips of the vines. You can also do this with vining squash and pumpkins.

Prune woody perennials, such as blueberries and gooseberries, and fruit trees, such as apples and pears, to shape them to fit your space and improve the air circulation around their branches. A yearly trimming of raspberry canes will encourage new growth that produces more fruit.

Ornamental vines can quickly grow out of control. Clematis, for example, can grow to an immense size in a single growing season. Wisteria tends to grow more slowly, but will need cutting back so it doesn't block windows or doors.

Whenever you prune or pinch back plants, dispose of the cuttings or add them to your compost pile rather than leave them in your garden where the dying foliage will invite pests and encourage disease. Also, remember never to put diseased leaves and stems in your compost; dispose of them separately.

How to Compost

Compost is created when bacteria decompose plant matter. Composting not only allows you to dispose of plant and kitchen waste but also to turn that waste into a rich soil that's full of micronutrients. You can use compost to fill your containers or as a top dressing to provide extra nutrition to your plants.

The ideal way to combine plant matter in a compost pile is by layering brown and green waste. Green waste includes kitchen scraps, weeds that haven't gone to seed, green leaves, and grass clippings. (Avoid composting large quantities of acidic fruit, as they can make the pH level of the compost too acidic for your plants.) Tea bags, coffee grounds, and eggshells can also be included; crush eggshells before adding, so they'll break down more quickly. Meat and dairy products are not recommended, as they're particularly attractive to pests, such as rats and racoons. Brown waste includes cardboard, hay, dry leaves, straw, and other clean paper waste.

When these two types of waste are layered, they provide the right balance of carbon and nitrogen for bacteria to break down the waste efficiently. A well-maintained compost bin can create usable compost in as little as three to four weeks. If you're not able to add different types of waste regularly, you'll still make compost—it will simply take more time and more regular turning.

The bacteria in a compost pile will decompose waste quickly and without emitting an odor if they receive ideal amounts of oxygen and moisture. Turning a compost pile will help introduce more oxygen into your pile and help regulate its moisture content. In an ideal world, your compost pile should be turned once or twice a week to encourage rapid decomposition. This can be tricky, particularly if your compost container or pile is large. If this is the case, you might want to use a compost turner or aerator or a garden fork to loosen up the pile, so the bacteria in the pile will get enough oxygen. If your pile has become too wet and compacted, add a few shovels of garden soil or shredded newspaper, in addition to turning and loosening it, to help restart the decomposition process. Sufficient moisture will usually be supplied from the produce you add, but if the pile starts to dry out, you can pour some water over the top of it.

Although a well-maintained compost bin or pile shouldn't smell, it's not often easy to work a compost bin properly and some smell is typical. Try to position it as far as you can from doors and seating areas.

Making Compost Tea

Compost tea is made by soaking homemade or commercial compost in water. It's suitable for any plant, can be used any time of the year, and is often used by championship growers as their secret sauce for growing prize-winning plants.

Place a shovelful of compost in a five-gallon bucket, cover with water, and stir to mix. Cover the bucket and set aside for three to four days, stirring the mixture once or twice a day to encourage the nutrients in the compost to dissolve into the water. Strain off the resulting liquid to use on your plants. Alternatively, you can place the compost in a burlap bag or tie it up in some permeable weed cloth before putting it in the bucket. The remaining solids can be used as mulch or returned to your compost pile.

You can use undiluted compost tea on established plants that are in the ground, but dilute the tea if you plan to use it on young seedlings or plants in containers. The recommended dilution rate is one part compost tea to ten parts water. Also use this dilution if you're planning to use the tea as a spray on foliage. Add a little vegetable oil to the mixture, which will help the tea stick to the leaves. Foliar sprays are best used first thing in the morning, so the leaves will get a chance to dry. Minerals in the tea may damage delicate leaves if the leaves haven't absorbed them before exposure to the strong summer sun. Leaves that are frequently damp overnight can be susceptible to diseases such as powdery mildew.

The effectiveness of compost tea relies on beneficial bacteria, and these bacteria can't survive for very long suspended in water. For this reason, use compost tea within a day or two after straining.

You can make compost in anything from a large plastic container to a homemade wooden or metal structure. If a compost pile proves to be too unsightly or unruly or requires too much effort to turn, a compost tumbler can be a great solution. With a turn of its handle, the tumbler will rotate the compost in the

bin, breaking it down more quickly. Although they do work if you tumble a little waste material at a time, they're more efficient when you have a full bin to turn.

Never compost diseased or pest-infested plant material, as it might encourage more disease or pest growth that could spread to your plants. Cat or dog waste can also introduce harmful bacteria into your compost. There's great debate even among scientists about how safe it is to compost animal manure, even from animals not raised for food. Animals raised in feedlots and fed the crushed remnants of other animals (yes, it happens) can be more likely to pass E. coli and salmonella in their manure, but there's no absolute guarantee that manure from non-feed animals will be completely safe. Know your manure sources, turn your pile as frequently as you can, and add in green waste, such as grass clippings, to increase the heat of your pile and destroy pathogens.

Pests and Diseases

Any plants, whether grown indoors or outside, may attract pests or contract diseases, but a vertical garden can provide some protection. You'll have more control over the soil your plants grow in, especially if you start out with a good-quality soil mix like the one on page 52. A number of pests and diseases are introduced through soil, so having a clean medium in the beginning will get you off on the right foot. If a fruit or vegetable touches the ground, it can contract a soil-borne disease or be damaged by soil pests. There are a number of common pests that don't like to climb, so plants in a vertical garden will be beyond their reach. Elevated containers will certainly discourage damage by burrowing rodents and voracious rabbits! It will also be easier for you to examine your plants if you don't have to bend over and hunt at ground level.

However, growing vertically won't protect your plants against every possible contamination or invasion. Flying or climbing pests will seek out your garden no matter how high it is. Certain plant diseases are wind borne, notably blight, which affects night-shades (eggplants, peppers, potatoes, and tomatoes).

Look over your plants regularly, and learn how to spot and manage problems. The best time to check your plants is while you water. Do a quick check under leaves and at the joints between the stems and leaves for any signs of a problem. Watch out for discoloration, wilting leaves, curling edges, or other damage to the plant that will indicate you need to give it a closer inspection. Catching problems early on makes them much easier to deal with, and it gives the plant more chance for survival. Finally, practice good garden hygiene. Keep your garden clear of debris, and allow plenty of room around plants for air to circulate.

PESTS

The majority of pests can be removed by hand if you catch them before they become too numerous, though you may want to use gloves rather than your bare hands. Some people don't like

touching pests, and some pests, such as certain hairy caterpillars, can cause an allergic reaction. Others will be too small to pick off, and for those I recommend one of my ideas for sprays on page 79.

Three of the most common garden pests are aphids, slugs, and snails. Aphids are tiny white bugs that gather on new growth and other tender parts of a plant. They can be picked off and crushed between your fingertips, but with large or persistent infestations, spray the undersides of leaves with a garden hose. Use as strong a stream to dislodge them as you can without damaging leaves. Ants will often farm aphids for the nectar they produce and kill or drive off natural predators of aphids, so you may also have to take care of an ant problem too.

Slugs and snails are particularly problematic in mild, humid climates (such as in England where I live). They can reach plants no matter how high a vertical garden is located because they're extremely good climbers, and they're voracious eaters. There are plenty of folk remedies for repelling them, such as using copper bands or crushed eggshells around your plants, but none of these tricks are particularly effective. Slug pellets work, but they can be harmful to other animals and wildlife.

In some cases, they can leach toxins into the soil, which are then absorbed by your plants.

From my experience, the most effective ways to deal with slugs are by putting out beer traps and by handpicking them off the plants. Place small containers of beer on the ground around and below your plants. Slugs will be attracted to the smell, crawl into the containers, and drown. (You don't have to use pricey beer; slugs aren't fussy and will happily drown in a cheap beer.) This method won't entirely rid your area of slugs, and the slug-beer mixture can develop an unpleasant aroma, particularly in hot weather.

The second, and most effective, method is to pick the critters off by hand and destroy them. It's more time-consuming, but it works. Slugs tend to come out when it's damp or at dusk, so this is the best time to collect them.

I use a combination of these methods, putting beer traps around my plants, then picking off slugs two or three times a week. This isn't 100 percent effective, but it does keep them under control without taking up a great deal of my time.

Slugs and snails love to hide, so that pile of leaf debris or the upturned plant pot in the corner of your garden could be harboring these sneaky pests. If you keep your garden tidy and remove possible hiding places, you will reduce their numbers significantly. Also, look out for their eggs, which look like clusters of white balls laid on or just under the soil. These can be disposed of or left out in the open where a predator can find them.

DISEASES

Plant diseases can be more challenging to treat than pest invasions because each disease requires a different approach. Some diseases are so difficult to manage that, more often than not, your plant will succumb no matter what you do.

The best insurance against diseased plants is to follow a few easy practices. If you use the same soil in the same containers year after year, you will find that diseases will build up in that soil. If at all possible, change your soil every year or at least change the top couple of inches. If you start having problems with diseases, change out the soil in your containers and sterilize the containers before reusing them. Avoid putting the same plants in the same containers year after year unless you clean the containers thoroughly. This will decrease the risk of spreading soil-borne diseases that are particular to those plants. If you compost, never put any diseased plant material in your compost pile, as you can spread the disease when you use the compost. Always destroy diseased plant material or throw it in the trash.

One of the most common diseases is powdery mildew, which particularly affects broad-leaf plants, such as squashes and pumpkins. It can be triggered when leaves can't dry out properly. Typically, this occurs when plants are watered from above instead of at soil level or the plants don't have enough space between them for air to circulate. If you water at the base of the plants rather than the leaves, not only will your plants stay dry, they will get more water. Mildew can also occur when the leaves of your plants get wet in the evening, either from watering or rain. Damp nights encourage mildew growth. If you have affected plants, be sure to check any plants that are above them; they may also have mildew and may be spreading it to plants below.

A common problem of tomatoes or potatoes is blight, an airborne disease that can be treated if you catch it early enough. However, it will spread very quickly and will be harmful to both plants and fruits. If potatoes have matured, you can remove the stems and leaves and keep the potatoes underground until you're ready to use them. It's much more difficult to deal with blighted tomatoes. You have to be very diligent about remov-

ing afflicted leaves. Your best bet with both tomatoes and potatoes is to buy blight-resistant varieties, which will provide you some protection.

TREATMENTS

There are chemical sprays you can use to treat diseased or pest-ridden plants, but you should also consider going organic. Organic methods are better for you, your plants, and the environment. Toxins from chemical treatments will build up in your soil, more so in containers than in open ground. If you're using a spray on edible crops, ensure it's suitable for them, as not all sprays are. Although I recommend that organic sprays be your first port of call, you may need to use nonorganic products for serious infestations.

You can make up an organic spray that's effective on a wide variety of plants by blending a bulb of garlic with a teaspoon of cayenne in a quart of water. Let it sit for about an hour, then strain through cheesecloth. Add a tablespoon of liquid dish soap, mix well, and apply to plants first thing in the morning.

Two other organic pest and disease control methods are companion planting and the introduction of beneficial insects. Companion plants have properties that will repel pests or prevent or minimize the impact of disease in other plants. You can plant marigolds near tomatoes, which will act to deter blight and keep it from spreading. Radishes will help repel cucumber beetles. There are also beneficial insects you can purchase online, including native ladybugs and praying mantises, both of which will make short work of aphids.

Best Wishes for Success

By now you should have the information you need to set up and grow a vertical garden. Although there are good practices to follow and tricks to use, the bottom line is plants want to grow! All you have to do is provide soil, sunlight, and water to realize a bountiful harvest from a small area.

Now it's time for you to start planning your vertical garden and put those plans into place. There are so many ways to make your space come alive. Let your creativity loose, and your plants will reward you.

ABOUT JASON

Jason Johns has been a keen gardener for over twenty years, having taken on numerous weed-infested patches and turned them into productive vegetable gardens. One of his first gardening experiences was digging up an entire plot that was four hundred square feet and turning it into a vegetable garden—much to the delight of his neighbors, who all got free vegetables! It was through this experience that he discovered his love of gardening and started to learn more about the subject.

Jason's first encounter with greenhouse gardening resulted in a tomato-infested jungle, but he soon learned how to grow a wide variety of plants—from grapes to squashes to tomatoes and much more—in his greenhouse. (To his wife's delight, the window sills in their house are no longer filled with seed trays every spring.) He also loves to grow giant and unusual vegetables and is still planning on breaking the four-hundred-pound barrier with one giant pumpkin.

Jason is passionate about helping people learn to grow their own fresh produce and enjoy the many benefits that come with it, from the exercise involved in gardening to the nutrients found in freshly picked produce. He often says that when you've tasted a freshly picked tomato, you'll never want to buy another one from a store again!

He's also very active in the personal development community, having written self-help books on subjects such as motivation and confidence. Jason is a qualified clinical hypnotist and has recorded over eighty hypnosis programs, which are all available from his website: musicforchange.com.

For more great gardening tips and advice, you can visit Jason at owninganallotment.com.

Click on the contact link to request his free newsletter and get notifications about his new books, as well as coupons good for 20 percent off any of the training offered.

See Jason's video diary at youtube.com/owninganallotment.

Join Jason on Facebook at facebook.com/owninganallotment.

Find Jason on Twitter and Instagram as @allotmentowner.

INDEX

elevation and, 74
fruits and, 11, 41
height of plants and, 10, 14
pipe cleaners for, 39–40
slugs/snails and, 3, 11, 14
step stools/ladders for, 68
when feeding, 68
when transplanting, 60
when watering, 64, 68
wind and, 14, 28, 42, 49
dill, 13–14
diseases
   access to garden and, 28
   advantages of vertical gardening
     and, 74
   air circulation and, 31, 40
   blight, 78–79
   as challenging, 77
   compost/compost tea and, 70,
     72, 73, 77
   obtaining advice about, 26
   plant damage and, 68
   powdery mildew, 78
   soil and, 50, 77
   treating, 79–80
   watering and, 64
   as wind-borne, 75
drip irrigation systems, for
   watering, 64, 65–66

E
eggplants, 25, 31, 75
epic vertical gardens, 6

F
feeding plants, 51, 68–69
fennel, supports for, 13–14
ferns, *20, 54*
fertilizer, 53, 69
flowers/flowering plants
   access to garden and, 29
   choosing, 24
   fruits/vegetables and, 5
   grouping, 17

ornamental, 16, 20
siting, 27
starting from seed, 58
supports and, 33
wind and, 42
fruit trees, 15, 58, *70*
fruits. *See also* individual types of
   access to garden and, 29
   as attractive, 5
   blight and, 78
   choosing, 14–15, 17, 24, 25
   size of and, 10–11
   supports and, 11, 36, 40–41,
     49
   wind and, 42
fungus/fungal diseases, 31, 64

G
garlic, *18,* 79
geraniums, *20*
gooseberries, *17, 70*
grapes
   about, 17
   climbing height and, 10
   in containers (planters), 15
   pergolas and, 39
greenhouses
   to extend growing season, 25
   hydroponic growing and, 6
   to increase growing space, 2
   for protection, 24
   seedlings started in, 57, 58
grow lights, for indoor living wall
   plants, *54–55*
growing season, climate and, 25,
   30–31
gutters/drainpipes, as containers,
   45–47

H
happiness, when gardening, *3*
height of plants, 10, 26, 27
herbs. *See also* specific types of
   choosing, 13–14, 21

in hanging baskets, 45
in living wall indoors, *54–55*
siting, 32
honeysuckle, supports for, 33, 34
hostas, *20*
hydroponics, indoor living wall
and, *55*

I

impatiens, *20*
indoor living wall, *54–55*
insects for pest/disease control, 80
irrigation
automatic irrigation systems,
28, 45, 61, 64–66
for gutter/drainpipe containers,
45, 47
liquid feeds in, 69
rain barrel for, 63
ivy, *20*

J

jasmine, supports for, 33, 34

K

kiwi, *17*

L

ladybugs, as beneficial, 80
lavender, 13, *21*
leaf burn, 69
leeks, 12, *18*
lemon balm, *21*
lettuce
about, 18
climate and, 25
containers (planters) and, 48,
51
in epic vertical gardens, 6
as shallow-rooted, 11
siting, 26, 27, 31
space for, 23
sun exposure and, 26
as wind-tolerant, 28

liquid feeds, 69
living wall indoors, *54–55*
lobelia, 16
loganberries, 15

M

Malaysian vertical gardens, 6
manure
chicken manure, as feed, 49,
53, 69
compost and, 73
marjoram, *21, 32*
melons
about, 17
choosing, 41
climate and, 25
as desirable, 11
supports and, 11, 40
mint, *21*
mobility/back problems, vertical
gardening and, 7
mold, air circulation and
supports and, 37, 40, 50
water and, 31

N

nasturtiums, *20*
nettles, as organic feed, 69

O

onions, 11, 12, *18*
oregano, 14, *21, 32*
organic feeds, 69
organic sprays, for pests/diseases,
79–80
ornamental plants
about, 16–17
flowers, 20
fruits, 17
herbs, 21
vegetables, 18–19

P

pallets, as supports, 37–38

pansies, *20*
parsley, *21, 31, 32*
parsnips, 12, *18*
passion flower, 16
passion fruit, *17*
paths in gardens, 29, 50
pear trees, pruning, *70*
peas
    about, 19
    advantages for, 11–12
    as attractive, 5
    choosing, 9
    in hanging baskets, 45
    soil and, 53
    supports for, 35
peat moss, soil and, 52
peppers
    about, 19
    blight and, 75
    choosing, 25
    siting, 31
pergolas/arbors/arches, 38–39, 45
perlite, 46, 66
pests
    about, 75–77
    common, 76
    companion planting and, 80
    compost and, 70, 71, 73
    elevation and, 74
    hidden, 77
    obtaining advice about, 26
    rain barrels and, 64
    removing, by hand, 75–76, 77
    siting plants and, 28
    soil and, 51, 74
    supports and, 41
    treating, 79–80
    watering and, 64
pet waste, compost and, 73
phosphorous, in commercial
        feeds, 69
pineberries, as shallow-rooted, 14
pipe cleaners, for attaching
        plants, 39–40

planters. *See* containers (planters)
plastic soda bottle, for watering,
        66, *67*
potassium, in commercial feeds,
        69
potatoes
    about, 19
    blight and, 75, 78–79
    succession planting and, 31
powdery mildew, 64, *72,* 78
praying mantises, as beneficial,
        80
premade containers, 48
primroses, *20*
pruning, *70*
pumpkins
    advantages of growing
        vertically, 4
    feeding, 68
    powdery mildew and, 78
    pruning, *70*
    supports and, 11, 36, 40, 41

R
radishes
    about, 19
    companion planting and, 31,
        80
    pruning, as not necessary, 70
    as shallow-rooted, 11, 12, 43
rain barrels/rainwater collection,
        28, *64*
raspberries, 15, *17, 70*
red currants, 15
red onions, 11
rocket (arugula), *18*
roots of plants. *See also* specific
        types of plants
    container planting and, 30
    depth of, 10
    drainage holes and, 43–44
    drip irrigation systems and, 66
    hydroponic growing and, 55
    seedlings and, 60

My garden is
my most beautiful
masterpiece.

CLAUDE MONET

CANNING AND PRESERVING AT HOME

A Complete Guide to Canning, Preserving and Storing Your Produce

978-1545202401 • 192 pages • $2.99

COMPANION PLANTING SECRETS

Healthy Crops, Higher Yields, Natural Pest & Disease Control

978-1548374754 • 116 pages • $8.95

COMPOSTING MADE EASY

A Complete Guide to Composting at Home

978-1985772304 • 101 pages • $2.99

CONTAINER GARDENING

Growing Fruits and Vegetables in Small Places

978-1517597214 • 74 pages • $7.99

COOKING WITH ZUCCHINI

Delicious Recipes, Preserves and More with Courgettes

978-1974056316 • 128 pages • $2.99

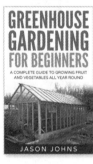

GREENHOUSE GARDENING FOR BEGINNERS

A Complete Guide to Growing Fruit and Vegetables All Year Round

978-1539126195 • 159 pages • $9.99

GROWING FRUIT

The Complete Guide to Growing Fruit at Home

978-1502315816 • 138 pages • $7.78

GROWING GARLIC

The Complete Guide to Growing, Harvesting, Storing & Using Garlic

978-1544042701 • 86 pages • $7.99

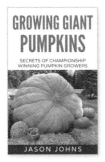

GROWING GIANT PUMPKINS

Secrets of Championship
Winning Pumpkin Growers

978-1511470384 • 86 pages • $8.99

HOW TO GROW POTATOES

The Guide to Choosing, Planting and
Growing in Containers or the Ground

978-1537555645 • 86 pages • $7.99

HYDROPONIC GARDENING

A Beginner Guide to Growing
Plants at Home without Soil

978-1502525857 • 80 pages • $7.99

INDOOR GARDENING

The Complete Guide to Growing Herbs,
Flowers, Vegetables & Plants
in Your House

978-1977592972 • 168 pages • $8.99

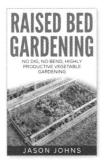

RAISED BED GARDENING

No Dig, No Bend, Highly Productive
Vegetable Gardening

978-1517138356 • 92 pages • $8.99

SQUARE FOOT GARDENING

Low Maintenance, No Dig
Growing More in Less Space

978-1537419121 • 54 pages • $7.99

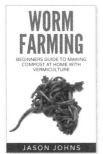

WORM FARMING

Beginners Guide to Making Compost
at Home with Vermiculture

978-1508687429 • 62 pages • $7.99

GROUNDSWELL BOOKS
SOLUTIONS FOR A SUSTAINABLE WORLD

For more books that inspire readers to create a healthy,
sustainable planet for future generations, visit
BookPubCo.com

The Garden Seed Saving Guide
Third Edition
Easy Heirloom Seeds
for the Home Gardener
Jill Henderson
978-1-57067-346-7 • $9.95

How to Start a Worm Bin
Your Guide to Getting Started
with Worm Composting
Henry Owen
978-1-57067-349-8 • $9.95

Automating Hydroponics
For Kitchen Gardeners
to Greenhouse Growers
Cerreto Rossouw
978-1-57067-366-5 • $14.95

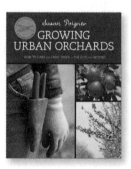

Growing Urban Orchards
How to Care for Fruit Trees
in the City and Beyond
Susan Poizner
978-1-57067-352-8 • $19.95

Purchase these titles from your favorite book source or buy them directly from:
Book Publishing Company • PO Box 99 • Summertown, TN 38483 • 1-888-260-8458
Free shipping and handling on all orders